The Freud Lectures at Yale University

Psychoanalysis
and the History of the Individual

by Hans W. Loewald, M.D.

New Haven and London, Yale University Press, 1978

*Designed by Thos. Whitridge
and set in IBM Aldine Roman type.
Printed in the United States of America by
The Murray Printing Company, Westford, Mass.*

*Published in Great Britain, Europe, Africa, and Asia
(except Japan) by Yale University Press, Ltd., London.
Distributed in Latin America by Kaiman & Polon, Inc.,
New York City; in Australia and New Zealand by Book &
Film Services, Artarmon, N.S.W., Australia; and in Japan
by Harper & Row, Publishers, Tokyo Office.*

Library of Congress Cataloging in Publication Data

*Loewald, Hans W   1906–
   Psychoanalysis and the history of the individual.*

   *(The Freud lectures at Yale University)
   1. Psychoanalysis—Addresses, essays, lectures.
2. Developmental psychology—Addresses, essays, lectures.
I. Title. II. Series: Yale University. The Freud lectures at
Yale University.
BF173.L567   1978   150'.19'5   77–11992
ISBN 0–300–02172–0*

The Freud Lectures at Yale University are supported by the Mark and Viva Kanzer Fund established in 1974 by Mark Kanzer, M.D., to promote scholarly exchange between psychoanalysis and the humanities.

Contents

Preface   ix

I Man as Moral Agent   1

II Transference and Love   27

III Comments on Religious Experience   53

Preface

I am deeply grateful to the Advisory Committee of the Kanzer Fund for having asked me to present these lectures. The Mark and Viva Kanzer Fund, thanks to the devotion of Dr. Mark Kanzer to psychoanalysis, to humanistic scholarship, and to Yale University, was created for the purpose of keeping alive and illuminating the bonds between psychoanalysis and the humanities— bonds that are inherent in the creation of psychoanalysis itself and derive from the original unity of human knowledge and from a common concern for the life of the mind.

I welcome the opportunity to present some facets of psychoanalytic research and psychoanalytic theory to an interdisciplinary readership. It requires language which is less technical than that called for in addressing an audience restricted to professional psychoanalysts. I hope that such language will clarify, rather than distort, the meaning of technical concepts and terms and will permit the reader to place psychoanalytic findings and ideas within a broader framework. At the same time, a broader audience challenges me to attend to and articulate some of the wider humanistic and philosophical implications of psychoanalysis and its influence on modern life and contemporary sensibility.

Following a few more general observations, in the first two lectures I deal with some aspects of man as a moral agent and of man's love life. In the third lecture I discuss certain phases of religious experience that psychoanalytic psychology so far has considered only tangentially and with misgivings.

I am grateful to Yale University Press for their generous support, and particularly to Jane Isay for her dedicated and expert editing work.

I
Man as Moral Agent

These lectures are dedicated to the memory of Sigmund Freud. His work as a physician exploring and treating people's troubled minds, and as an innovator in the understanding of the mind, still inspires us today: not only those of us who have chosen psychoanalysis as a profession, a domain, and a method of psychological research, and not only psychiatrists and allied professionals, but also many scholars working in the area of the humanities. I hardly need to mention the pervasive influence Freud's discoveries and ideas continue to exert on the world at large.

According to a recent Program Announcement by the National Endowment for the Humanities, the humanities include the following fields: "history, philosophy, languages, linguistics, literature, archeology, jurisprudence, history and criticism of the arts, ethics, comparative religion, and those aspects of the social sciences employing historical and philosophical approaches." The following significant comment is added:

Because man's experience has been principally preserved through books, art works, and other cultural objects, the humanities are often defined in terms of specific academic disciplines. However, the concerns of the humanities extend, through the classroom, the library, and the media, to encompass a host of social, ethical, and cultural questions which all human beings confront throughout the course of their lives. The humanities thus comprise the family of knowledge that deals with what it has been—and is—to be human, to make value judgments, and to select the wiser course of action. This is achieved primarily through the examination of human experience and its implications for the present and the future.[1]

It may be permissible, even desirable, in speaking to an interdisciplinary audience, occasionally to move back and forth among several languages or terminologies, with the hope that words and concepts used in different disciplines thus may gain in meaning and illuminate each other. But I am aware of the risk that by doing so the phenomena at issue may appear more complex and ambiguous than when considered only from a single perspective.

I have given an indication of the range and scope of what are called "the humanities." Psychoanalysis may be described as a method of psychological investigation and treatment of the person and of personality disorders, as a body of knowledge and theory of the mind of the individual and its development, and as a unique

1. National Endowment for the Humanities, Program Announcement, 1975–1976, pp. 1 f. U.S. Government Printing Office, 1976.

process of human interaction. Psychoanalysis is centrally concerned with "what it has been and is to be human" and with "the examination of human experience and its implications for the present and the future." Since this is true, then psychoanalysis may be seen as belonging to the family of knowledge that deals with these questions, that is, to the humanities. But Freud and many of his followers also claim that it is a natural science. And it also is, by its origin and its specialized function in society, a medical or therapeutic art.

Let us admit that psychoanalysis, for the time being, is a rather untidy discipline, still feeling its way. In part this may be attributed to its youth—eighty-odd years is a short span in the life of a new discipline. But I believe that this untidiness, as compared with the more neatly defined areas and boundaries of other disciplines, is essentially a sign of the thrust of psychoanalysis in the direction of a new—and very old—unity of knowledge to which the most original minds in the sciences and other fields aspire today: an envisioned unity within multiplicity, whereby even such traditional dichotomies as those between theory and practice, between body and mind, between the natural and the mental sciences, are newly questioned.

The psychoanalytic process—advisedly I do not make a distinction here between investigation and treatment—and psychoanalytic findings and theory, are prominently concerned with man as a moral being. We only have to think of the role played in psychoanalysis by such problems and concepts as inner conflict, anxiety, guilt and shame, the superego, and the antagonism between the exigencies of societal and instinctual life. At the same time psychoanalysis deals prominently with man's love life; think of its emphasis on sexuality and of the central importance of transference in its various meanings and ramifications. Religious life, although viewed by Freud from a narrow and biased standpoint, has been another important subject of psychoanalytic research. These themes show how wide a net psychoanalysis casts in its search for an understanding of human nature. It would be false to claim that it is a biological science in any traditional sense of the word "biology."

It is the scope of psychoanalysis to consider human nature in the fullness of the individual's concrete existence and covering the full range of human potentialities, with special attention given—for a variety of reasons—to its historicity. The dimension of time plays an ever-increasing part in man's attempts to organize, master, and understand reality—be it the material reality of physics, chemistry, astronomy, and geology, or biological reality, or the reality of human history, its civilizations and societies, or of the individual person. This trend is connected with a deep modern interest in the nature of reality as process—in contrast to a substantive, static view—and with a pervasive tendency to understand what appears permanent and definitively structured in terms of the dynamics of becoming, that is, to reconstruct structures.

Psychoanalysis deals with man within the full range of his human potential. As to the somatic events and levels of human functioning, traditionally considered the domain of biology and physiology, psychoanalysis attempts to deal with them from a different viewpoint or within a larger context or framework—as being integrants, constituents, of the psychological organization of human beings, and as such affected by that organization.

Freud, in one of his last attempts to formulate "Some Elementary Lessons in Psychoanalysis" (written in London in 1938), repeated that psychology is a natural science (*eine Naturwissenschaft*). What else could it be? he asks.[2] The form of the question is the same as that of another question he asked when discussing the issue of moral responsibility for the content of dreams. Of course, he says, one must hold oneself responsible for one's evil dream impulses—what else would one do with them? (1925).[3] He takes for granted, in both instances, that there are no alternatives. But if the psychology that Freud created is a natural science, then we are dealing with concepts of nature and science that include man's moral nature, no less than his biological functions and processes, as topics for the scientific study of "nature." We shall see later in what sense man may be said to be responsible for his unconscious

2. *The Standard Edition of the Complete Psychological Works of Sigmund Freud* (hereafter cited as S.E.). London: The Hogarth Press and the Institute of Psycho-Analysis, 23:282.

3. *S.E.,* 19:133.

impulses; but in any case the psychoanalytic concept of moral responsibility appears to be different from the traditional one which is based on the consciousness of one's acts, thoughts, and intentions.

As to science, Freud wishes to emphasize that it is both possible and necessary to observe and investigate (with the same attitude of detached objectivity and unprejudiced wonderment used in physics) those phenomena of human life that we call man's higher functions, such as his moral or spiritual life. These functions and behaviors were traditionally regarded as too exalted or profound for scientific study, even as they appear to separate man from animal life. It is this specifically unprejudiced, objective attitude that for Freud characterizes the scientific spirit and method of approach, and not experiments and measurements in themselves. This method of approach can and must be used in the study of man's moral or love life, for example, no less than in the study of physiological processes, if the particular object of psychoanalysis, the human individual, is to be studied scientifically.

For Freud psychoanalysis was a natural science, first and foremost insofar as mental life is grounded in the physiological-biological reality of the human body. Instincts, *Triebe,* he tended to see as biological forces, but he also described them as mental representatives of such forces. The ontological status of mental representatives, of course, has remained unclear.

Freud hesitated to attribute reality to the mind and

contented himself with calling the psychical a "particular form of existence" (*eine besondere Existenzform*), not to be confused with material or "factual" reality. He admitted that he did not further pursue the question of psychic reality.[4] What in his view tends to confer a reality-like character on psychic life is the undeniable fact of the power of the unconscious.

Here he also speaks of the question of responsibility. This responsibility is not tied to the idea of good and evil, to moral values, but to the fact that the power of the unconscious or id is part of myself, and neither is of divine origin nor comes from alien spirits. Nevertheless, there is something daemonic about the id, something about the dynamic unconscious that is, as in the Greek idea of *daimon,* neither attributable to the power of a personal god, nor a powerful force of the person *qua* individual or conscious being, but something in between, having an impersonal character. The dynamic unconscious, for Freud the true psychic reality, is prior to conscious mentation and transcends the conscious personality. It not only engenders the formation of conscious mentation, but also determines conscious aspects of the life course, actions, and thoughts of the adult person.

The concept of science in its modern sense seems to be complementary to the concept of nature as objectified, distanced reality. Insofar as man can stand at a distance from himself, can objectively study not only

4. *The Interpretation of Dreams* (1900). *S.E.,* 5:620.

his own conscious actions and processes but the underlying unconscious processes that somehow lead to and
determine conscious life—to that extent psychoanalysis
can be a natural science. At the same time, the closeness of instinctual life to biological life was for Freud
a powerful argument in favor of seeing psychoanalysis
as a natural science, even when it came to investigate
the most distant derivatives of unconscious mentation,
as in ego-psychology.

From such a viewpoint, unconscious processes are
comparable to the atomic and subatomic processes
that underlie and compose the manifest structures and
processes of the physical world, or to the biochemical
and biophysical processes underlying the biological
world. Indeed, the knowledge of unconscious processes
and forces appears to have a simultaneously destructive
and creative potential similar to that of atomic physics,
or of biochemistry. On the other hand, as will become
more apparent (and again comparable perhaps to problems in modern physics), increased understanding of
unconscious mentation raises complex problems about
the idea of objectivity itself. It is as though the idea
and possibility of objective distance, of scientific objectivity, is inextricably interwoven with, or based on,
conscious mental processes.

I shall now proceed to consider the problem of
responsibility for one's unconscious and what I call
the moral implications of psychoanalysis. My main
concern is with what psychoanalysis, to my understand-

ing, implies about man's moral nature, and not with what psychoanalysis has contributed to the understanding of the origin of moral standards, the superego, guilt, and so forth. But a clear distinction between these issues is not always possible.

Freud has provided us with two formulations that indicate, from somewhat different angles, the direction and aim of psychoanalytic treatment: to make the unconscious conscious, and, "where id was ego shall come into being." Thus, the psychoanalytic process implies a conception of man's moral nature. Promoting the individual's consciousness, fostering his ego development, means—whatever else is conveyed by the terms consciousness and ego—promoting his taking responsibility for himself. The movement from unconscious to conscious experience, from the instinctual life of the id to the reflective, purposeful life of the ego, means taking responsibility for one's own history, the history that has been lived and the history in the making. In psychoanalysis, however, the emphasis is not only or primarily on the person's past history insofar as he consciously remembers it or can be told about by his elders. Psychoanalysis prominently is concerned with unconscious history. By this I mean not only the events of childhood and later life that have been forgotten. I mean that mass of past living and experiencing, which took place without self-awareness, and often— and this is more important—without the ego's mediation. The organizing activity of the ego is not necessarily in conscious awareness; in fact, it operates much of the time outside conscious awareness. It integrates raw experience, making it into a differentiated element of our psychic life, bringing it into a meaningful context. The idea of responsibility, in its most basic sense, then refers to that inner responsiveness to raw experience which is the hallmark of the ego and transposes raw experience onto a different plane.

Repression is a throwback to that older plane of experiencing: undesirable or unacceptable memories, thoughts, fantasies, by being excluded from ego organization, sink back to that raw form of mentation which is conceptualized as the dynamic unconscious or id.

Past history, then, is understood here not so much in the sense of past "objective" events or mental "contents," but more specifically in the sense of an earlier, archaic, form or level of mentation, an undifferentiated form of experiencing, that characterizes early developmental stages but is operative as well at chronologically later stages.

Let me emphasize again, before I go on, that my concern here is not with moral values, standards, or judgments. They of course may become the subject of analytic investigation, and the analyst's own moral standards may influence the treatment of his patients or his understanding of psychoanalytic psychology. But this is not the issue here. I am not speaking of specific moral or moralistic preoccupations and attitudes of patient or analyst, but of the fact that the dynamic unconscious or id is defined as capable of (or tending toward) a development in which unconscious forms of mentation may become integrated into a higher mental organization, or organized within a hierarchy of differentiated levels of mentation. This condition of higher organization is conceptualized as ego. The development in its direction is seen as being facilitated, perhaps even as originally brought about, by promoting conscious reflection.

A few very condensed remarks on conscious reflection: in a certain sense the expression is redundant. "Conscious" means being in a self-reflecting and self-reflected state. Reflection is a *con-scire,* a knowing-together. It represents the internalization of an interplay originally occurring between the infant and his or her primary caretaker, mostly the mother, and then recurring in many other relationships. Psychoanalysts have spoken of the mother, in the primordial infant–mother psychic unit, as a living mirror in which the infant gradually begins to recognize, to know himself, by being recognized by the mother. This recognition has much more than so-called cognitive connotations. It is mediated to the infant and growing child by a great variety of maternal activities and interactions with the child's bodily and instinctual life. Her knowing and understanding the child, as well as the imperfections and deficiencies of her understanding, are embedded in these interactions. This primal reflection and recognition brings about a *conscire* within the infant–mother

psychic matrix and gradually becomes a crucial constit-
uent, a potential of the individuating child's experiencing or mentation. Further complex developments, in
continuous interaction with the caring persons, lead to
that articulate and explicit conscire manifested in
language and eventually to conscience. The phenomenon of conscience is a more fully developed and
specialized resultant and function of what I call the
morality of mental development. The *con* in *conscire*—
the root verb for the words conscious and conscience
—expresses the belonging-together of, and internal
encounter between, "raw" experience and its reflecting
recognition by the other in oneself. The "other" in
oneself appears in psychoanalytic theory in such terms
as observing ego and superego. But this internal other
is only the end product of a complex differentiating—
from another viewpoint, self-alienating—process that
takes its start in the primary unity of the infant–mother
psychic matrix. This development constitutes the
individuation of the individual.

One further element in this process has to be made
explicit: the recognizing-caring activities of the primary
caretakers crucially contribute to the development of
the child's psychic life by the fact of their being ahead
of his present stage of organization. Parental caring,
knowing, understanding, embedded in their interactions
with the child, take place in the context and perspective
of the child's overall requirements and future course of
development, as perceived and misperceived by the

parents. Thus, parental recognizing care reflects more, as it were, to the child than what he presents; it mediates higher organization. This generation difference or gradient is essential. Similarly, the developing, internal conscire represents something other than an internal reflection of experience in the sense of mere "reduplication."

The id or dynamic unconscious, I have said, is the past history of the individual in the sense of being a mode of experience or mentation that is older than those forms of mental processes we are familiar with from conscious, rational life. We discern these primordial forms in early childhood, in the mental life of primitive peoples, in psychotics. We find signs and elements of it in dreams, in neurotic symptomatology, as well as in what we call the normal mental life of our waking state.

This "archaic" mode of mentation, however, is also a newly rediscovered and appreciated mode that is asserting its own validity and power in our culture. The discoveries, the thrust of psychoanalysis—almost against the conscious intentions of its creator—have contributed an important share to the new valuation of the irrational unconscious. In modern art, literature, and philosophy; in the mood, aspirations, conduct of life of the younger generation, we see a fresh flowering of that more ancient, more deeply rooted mode of human experience which perhaps is leading toward a less rigid, less frozen, and more humane rationality. Freud called the dynamic unconscious indestructible in comparison with the ephemeral and fragile, but infinitely precious, formations of consciousness. Where id was, there ego shall come into being. Too easily and too often ego is equated with rigid, unmodulated, and unyielding rationality. So today we are moved to add: where ego is, there id shall come into being again to renew the life of the ego and of reason.

Psychoanalytic theory distinguishes between the dynamic unconscious and preconscious mentation and demarcates the latter from conscious mentation in the strict sense, which involves conscious awareness. When I spoke of conscire, I had in mind, not conscious awareness, but the preconscious form of mentation. It is a conscire in its inner organization; but this form of mental process often is not in conscious awareness; and it is not necessarily consciously perceived. Since the term, *pre*conscious, stresses closeness or accessibility to conscious awareness, and since I believe that this is not the essential characteristic of the mental processes so designated, I prefer to speak of *conscient* processes. The term conscient intends to point out the structure of con-scire of this form of mental process. Conscient (preconscious) mentation loses the uniform single-mindedness of unconscious processes while gaining the new dimension of inner responsiveness involving a differentiation or dichotomy of a unitary mental activity. Such differentiation, which introduces duality and multiplicity into unity—and which may disrupt rather than articulate it—has its origin in, and is brought forth by, the caring environment's active mirroring. This mirroring, I said, reflects more than what the infant presents. It contains the mother's acts of organizing the infant's activities and experiences within an envisioned temporal-spatial totality of his being—the prototype of what is called his ego as a coherent organization. To the extent to which the infant's unitary (I am tempted to say, headlong) acts become integrated within such a totality, an internal mirroring comes into being. The totality or coherent organization is to begin with merely in the mother's foreseeing eye, as a kind of unperceived plan. And so the infant's uniform mental acts thus acquire differentiation.

Unconscious mentation lacks this differentiation. The *un-* in "unconscious" points out this privation. But it is a privation only in reference to conscient mentation. If uniform mentation is considered in its own right, the term "id" is more fitting, since it does not make reference to a conscire. Nevertheless, this uniform activity, although not a con-scire, is a *scire,* a form of knowing or "minding." When Freud included unconscious processes in the category of mental or psychic processes he made a decision. For a time he vacillated: should he treat them as biological or as psychological phenomena? Whatever their status, these processes *had* to be presumed. Only by postulating them could a number of mental and psychopathological phenomena be understood. Thus, Freud did not doubt the existence of such underlying processes. What was in doubt during his early work (and this echoes throughout his theorizing) was their status in the hierarchy of scientific study. In declaring them to be *psychic* processes, he took the step of investigating them from the standpoint of man's full mental life, from the perspective of man as a moral being, and not from the reductive perspective of modern natural science. But he never was wholly comfortable with his decision.

Early on, Freud equated the unconscious and the repressed, since his hypnotic and analytic studies showed that unconscious fantasies and memories at one time had been conscious. But at that time he did not yet distinguish between the dynamic unconscious and preconscious mentation, but only between mental processes in—and out of—awareness. It is significant that in the very beginning he felt that an unequivocally moral force, an effort of will on the part of the patient, was responsible for initiating repression. Later on, the dynamic unconscious was identified as a realm of mentality that developmentally precedes conscient (preconscious) and conscious mentation and forever remains the active, enduring origin and source for those more developed processes. What is repressed is drawn back into the archaic sphere of mentation, from whence it stems. This is an amoral realm, capable of being personalized.

Let me once more come back to the phrase: *Wo Es war, soll Ich werden;* where id was, there ego shall come into being. *Werden* is: to become, to come into being. *Soll* and "shall" indicate the setting of a task. If ego and conscient life mean higher mental organization, in the sense of evolving, then id would be ego *in statu nascendi*. The coming into being of higher organization, of a more complex, richer mentality, seen as the realization of a potentiality represented by the id, seems ordained, as it were, by the laws of evolution. Man is understood in psychoanalysis as tending toward higher organization, further development of his unconscious life forces. He tends to become a person. The development of a more conscious life involves a continuous appropriation of the unconscious levels of functioning, an owning up to them as potentially *me,* ego. This appropriation, this owning up, integrating the id into one's life context as an individual self, is then a developmental task or, in a different framework, an existential task. I believe that Heidegger's concepts of *Geworfenheit*—man is thrown into the world, unplanned and unintended by himself— and *Entwerfen*—the taking over and actively developing the potentialities of this fact—have grown in the same soil.[5]

5. The above is a vast oversimplification of Heidegger's extensive exposition of these concepts. His level of discourse and the intent of his quest for a philosophical elucidation of human existence (*Dasein*) are quite different from those of psychoanalysis as a psychological discipline. The factuality (*Geworfenheit*) of human existence in Heidegger's sense has a different dimension than the psychoanalytic id, and Heidegger does not concern himself with the differentiation of unconscious and conscious mentation. My comparison merely refers to the idea, which both authors have in common, epitomized in the dictum: Become what you are. Cf. Martin Heidegger, *Sein und Zeit.* Halle: Max Niemeyer Verlag, 1927, pp. 134 ff., 145 f.

To appropriate, to own up to, one's own history is
the task of psychoanalysis as a therapeutic endeavor. As
such it constitutes a resumption of psychic development, a resumption of developmental tasks. An important aspect of this process is remembering the past. But
much more is involved than recollection of past experiences and events, although such recollections
usually form significant stepping stones toward this
remembering.

Freud distinguished between remembering and repeating the past, only to claim immediately that repeating
the past is a form of remembering; it is an unconscious
form of remembering.[6] Repeating, in the sense of
re-enacting past experiences in the present, is remembering by action and affect rather than in thought. For
instance, childhood experiences with one's father are
re-enacted with a "father-figure" in adult life; they are
remembered in the form of similar or identical behavior
with the father-figure, but there is no recollection in
thought. A recollection in thought, capable of being
expressed in words, amounts to a restructuring of a
childhood memory on a higher level of mentation. We
may say that the unconscious memory, as such merely
expressed in action, has been lifted from that unconscious status into the status of consciousness—in the
psychoanalytic situation by the analyst's interpretation.
His interpretation—to the effect that the patient's

6. "Remembering, Repeating and Working Through" (1914).
S.E., 12:147-56.

behavior must represent the repetition of a childhood experience—brings the unconscious memory, reproduced in the here-and-now, into the context and on to the level of conscious thought. Under favorable circumstances, it enables the patient to connect or reconnect the two levels of mentation, to make the restructuring of the experience his own. We note that the analyst's interpretation is a form of active mirroring, reflecting back to the patient his behavior in a different light, in terms of higher, more comprehensive and more articulate mental organization—analogous to the parental mirroring function in infancy and childhood. Roughly speaking, the patient now may experience his interaction with the analyst/father-figure on two levels and may grasp that the dominance of the regressive level of mentation compelled him to re-enact experience as if he were back in the past.

To own up to our own history, to be responsible for our unconscious, in an important sense means, to bring unconscious forms of experiencing into the context and onto the level of the more mature, more lucid life of the adult mind. Our drives, our basic needs, in such transformation, are not relinquished, nor are traumatic and distorting childhood experiences made conscious in order to be deplored and undone—even if that were possible. They are part of the stuff our lives are made of. What is possible is to engage in the task of actively reorganizing, reworking, creatively transforming those early experiences which, painful as many of them have been, first gave meaning to our lives. The more we know what it is that we are working with, the better we are able to weave our history which, when all is said and done, is re-creating, in ever-changing modes and transformations, our childhood. To be an adult means that; it does not mean leaving the child in us behind.

There is no one-way street from id to ego. Not only do irrational forces overtake us again and again; in trying to lose them we would be lost. The id, the unconscious modes and contents of human experience, should remain available. If they are in danger of being unavailable—no matter what state of perfection our "intellect" may have reached—or if there is danger of no longer responding to them, it is our task as historical beings to resume our history making by finding a way back to them so that they may be transformed, and away from a frozen ego. This, I think, is the original and enduring quest of psychoanalysis, and its importance in modern history.

We modern Westerners are transfixed by the idea of development as progression in a straight line, as "progress." What is not progress is seen as stagnation, or worse, regression. In psychoanalysis the term "regression in the service of the ego"[7] had to be invented, in an attempt to do justice to the insight that ego development does not proceed in a straight line, does not con-

7. E. Kris, "The Psychology of Caricature." In *Psychoanalytic Explorations in Art.* New York: International Universities Press, 1952, p. 177.

sist in a movement further and further away from id.
Time, in human (not physical) terms, is not an arrow,
is not to be measured point by point. One might come
closer to human time by saying that it consists in an
interpenetration and reciprocal relatedness of past,
present, and future. The history of the individual, not
construed as the progression of external or intrapsychic
events during his life, is constituted by this more-or-less
actualized interpenetration and mutual determination of
the three temporal modes, as it unfolds during the
course of a life.

Pictured in physical, space-motion terms (more
adequately than by a straight line) individual development could be described as an ascending spiral in which
the same basic themes are re-experienced and enacted
on different levels of mentation and action. Sublimation
might best be understood in the light of such an image.

It will be objected that the superego should not be
absent from a psychoanalyst's discussion of moral issues.
So far I have not been explicit. If id and ego represent,
respectively, psychic past and present, the superego
might be seen as the representative of futurity. The
superego is conceptualized as the inner agency of standards, demands, ideals, hopes, reproaches, and punish-
ments. We become aware of it as the voice of conscience,
and in relation to it we may experience guilt, shame,
pride, or self-approval. It represents the care and concern we have for ourselves, in past and present, as
continuing on into a future that is to be shaped. The

superego has been characterized as a differentiating grade in the ego (*eine Stufe im Ich*).[8] In terms of psychic time, this is the differentiation between inner present and inner future in the course of mental development. It is the growing recognition of a differential between who I am, what I do at present, and who I may or should be, what I may, should or should not do in the future—as hoped for, desired, demanded, by myself. The foundation for this differentiating grade is laid in those early times, when the mother, as a living mirror, reflected "more" to the child than he presented, when she, in her responsive activities, was cognizant of his potential for future growth and development and mediated it to the infant.

The superego, as a differentiating grade or phase in the ego, is brought about by the internalization of the parents' acts of envisioning future development and exemplifying it. At the same time, Freud stressed the intimate relations of the superego to the id. I wish to point out only one aspect of this relationship that has bearing on my main theme. Freud alluded to it in a posthumous, unfinished book, "An Outline of Psychoanalysis" (1938).[9] In speaking of the relations between superego and id he quotes a line from Goethe's *Faust:* "What thou hast inherited from thy fathers, acquire it to make it thine." The past comprises the inherited,

8. S. Freud, "Group Psychology and the Analysis of the Ego" (1921). *S.E.*, 18:129.

9. *S.E.*, 23:207.

innate potential of our genes, the historical, cultural, moral tradition transmitted to us by our elders, and finally that primordial form of mentation, called unconscious or id, and the "contents" of our lives that are experienced in this primordial form at the earliest level. This past is to be acquired, appropriated, made ours, in the creative development of the future.

To the extent to which the individual remains entangled in his unappropriated id or disowns it, as in repression—and most of us do to a considerable extent— he is driven by unmastered unconscious forces within himself. He is free to develop, to engender his future, to the extent to which he remains or becomes open to his id and can personalize, again and again and on various levels, his unconscious powers. For Freud these unconscious powers are the true psychic reality. This apersonal ground of our existence, he claims, we are called upon to make human, to make, each in his own way, into a person.

Freud's last instinct theory postulates Eros and Thanatos, the love or life instinct and the destructive or death instinct, as those apersonal—and that also means, amoral—forces. They become more or less personalized in the conduct of a human life. Freud was not a religious man and certainly not a mystic. But one does not have to be a mystic to remain open to the mysteries of life and human individuality, to the enigmas that remain beyond all the elucidations of scientific explanation and interpretation. The life and death instinct theory was Freud's way of naming the creative-destructive powers that shape, and are shaped by, becoming a person.

Let me close with a quotation from Samuel Butler, another scientific spirit preoccupied with the unconscious, pertaining to science:

> If it tends to thicken the crust of ice on which, as it were, we are skating, it is all right. If it tries to find, or professes to have found, the solid ground at the bottom of the water, it is all wrong. Our [that is, the scientist's] business is with the thickening of this crust by extending our knowledge downward from above, as ice gets thicker while the frost lasts; we should not try to freeze upwards from the bottom.[10]

10. *The Note-Books of Samuel Butler,* selections arranged and edited by Henry Festing Jones. New York: Dutton, 1917, p. 329.

II

Transference and Love

Psychoanalysis has contributed to the understanding of man's love life, more specifically, of its genesis, development, and vicissitudes. What from a general point of view is genesis and development, becomes history in the unfolding of the individual. In the process of individuation the human being becomes historical. Historicity is understood here as that character of human experience which I called appropriation or owning up to one's past, to one's more or less unconscious motivational forces, to the "givens" of one's life. Taking over one's past, making it one's own, however, is not a return to the past in order to get lost in it. The past is important in view of and in relation to the present and future of one's life. Nostalgic reliving of youthful experiences, bitter reminiscing about past injuries and hurts, sad or angry complaints and accusations, or happy accounts of valued experiences and deeds—these and many other forms of evoking the past are ingredients, or steps, in the process of taking it over as one's own, in order to lead it into a future. The future, then, may have a chance to be my future, not the imitation of someone else's life, or merely the appendage of someone else, or a series of attempts to rebel or comply.

By the past in human life I do not just mean the mass of so-called contents of the mind, memories, or mental representations, of past experiences and events that may or may not be available for recall. The aspect of the mind's past I wish to discuss, in relation to love and historicity, is related to the theme of the first lecture. I am thinking of the modes of organization of experience that differ from those called preconscious, or conscient, and conscious mentation. The dynamic unconscious or id is not properly to be conceived as a region or province of the mind where archaic—we might say, prehistoric— memory contents are preserved, and where repressed memories come to be lodged, as a region of "mental contents" that is more or less inaccessible to consciousness. In its fundamental meaning, unconscious is the name for a mode of experiencing or mentation that continually, throughout life, constitutes the active base and source of more differentiated and more complexly organized modes of mentation. What I call my unconscious memories and impulses are potentially mine to the extent to which they may be raised to a new level of mentation, may become integrated with the context of my conscient mode of experiencing. Such appropriation is seen as a developmental, evolutionary thrust or tendency of humans. It is not a process that at some point in individual development comes to an end, but an ongoing activity, or one that is resumed again and again.

It would not do justice, however, to the complexity and richness of human life experience, if one only stressed the movement toward consciousness and over-looked or neglected the fact that we are dealing rather with a circularity or interplay between different levels of mentation. Formulated in terms of appropriation, it looks as if there is a need for conscient appropriation of unconscious experience as well as a need for re-appropriating conscient modes (and the corresponding mental contents) into unconscious mental activity— and back again toward consciousness. What counts is this live communication, a mutual shaping, a reciprocal conforming, of levels of mentation. The richer a person's mental life is, the more he experiences on several levels of mentation, the more translation occurs back and forth between unconscious and conscious experience. To make the unconscious conscious, is onesided. It is the *transference* between them that makes a human life, that makes life human.

The phenomenon, the concept of transference, is the key to the psychoanalytic approach to love. But I just spoke of transference between id and ego, be-tween unconscious and conscient modes and levels within the psyche. Generally one thinks of transference as something going on between people, and especially, in the psychoanalytic situation, as transference from the patient to the analyst. Popularly this is often taken to mean that the patient "falls in love" with the analyst, a notion—however simpleminded or naïve—that suggests the connection between transference and love.

I shall try to develop the thesis that the concept of transference opened up the historical dimension of man's love life while at the same time disclosing the erotic dimension of his individuation and historicity, of his becoming what may properly be called a self.

The concept of transference provides a scientific approach to the phenomenon of love: it helps to give us a deeper understanding of the genesis and the vicissitudes of love, to grasp the roots and motivations for the tangled web of heterosexual and homosexual passions and affectionate attachments in the course of a human life. It elucidates the infantile and unconscious sources and thereby the historical determinants of man's adult love life. At the same time, applied to the inner fabric of the psyche, the concept of transference illuminates the libidinal ("narcissistic") bonds that, once internalized, contribute to the dynamic organization of the individual as a self-appropriating, that is, historical being. Freud spoke of transference not only in regard to object-libidinal attachments, but also in regard to "the interplay of excitations between the preconscious and the unconscious,"[11] that is, in the context of intrapsychic transactions.

11. *The Interpretation of Dreams. S.E.*, 5:564. See also *ibid.*, 562–63.

—

Psychoanalysis distinguishes two forms of libido, object libido and narcissistic libido. In the early stages of psychoanalysis, attention was focused on object libido and its vicissitudes in the development of man's love life. Freud, to the dismay of his contemporaries (an attitude shared by many of our contemporaries), insisted on the existence of infantile sexuality. The facts of passionate, including physical-sexual, excitability, stimulation, involvement, in childhood are incontrovertible. Let us take for granted, also, that during the so-called oedipal phase of psychosexual development there is a first flowering of object-love, in the intimacy of the family mainly directed to parents and siblings, and that this constellation in many ways is the prototype for later love relations and object relations. Beginning with the oedipal stage, mother and father and siblings are, more than was the case before, experienced by the child as entities separate and different from himself. I am implying that the term "oedipal stage" refers not merely to instinctual and affective development but also to what we distinguish in psychic life as cognitive development. The two, however, are at that stage so intertwined, so interdependent, that it is hard to speak of them as two different lines of development. In any event, the child begins to experience his love objects as separate and different from himself. And it is in part their being different that makes them desirable. One could say just as well that it is the intensity of desire that conveys their being different.

Object libido, as distinguished from narcissistic libido, does not simply mean that, from an external observer's point of view, somebody else is desired, but that this somebody else is desired *as another person*. In object-libidinal acts another is constituted, experienced, as an object to whom one relates. In such a relatedness both oneself as subject and the other as object are established. Concretely speaking, this implies at least a minimal degree of awareness that there is some difference between the other's needs, desires, feelings, and one's own. The sense of needs and feelings being one's own, of being a subject, as distinguishable from an object, develops together with the sense of another's needs and feelings being *his* own. It is the same developmental step.

We see a baby suckling at the mother's breast. If we describe this as a spectacle, in terms of adult objectifying mentation like that of an ordinary outside observer, we would say that this is the first object relation of the infant. But what if we want to describe this event in terms of the infant's incipient mentation, of his psychic reality, and not in terms of the advanced mental level of an adult observer? The latter is like an instrument or method that is unfit for the purpose. If it is true, however, that the adult mind does not operate merely and at all times only on the level of objectifying mentation, that we are capable of experiencing on less differentiated and less complex mental levels (and indeed not infrequently do), then we may have a method of approaching primitively organized mental processes and gaining some insight into them. This nonobjective kind of knowledge is called empathic. Actually, I believe, we use it a great deal in our everyday relations with and understanding of other people, although we often do not notice it and it has not been adequately investigated. Therefore it seems more mysterious and unreliable than it is. Analysts, of course, although not eager to say much about it since it is likely to be called unscientific, use empathy a great deal in their work. All knowledge has its shortcomings and pitfalls; traditional objective observation, despite its successes in many fields, falls short of being adequate when it comes to unconscious mental processes. It distorts, by its objectifying methodology—inherent in the particular mental processes used in such observation—the phenomena to be understood. This is not to say that our unconscious mental processes, operating in empathic understanding, are an unfailing instrument—or that we know much about its workings. But every analyst knows that it does work many times and is indispensable.

To come back to the infant and his incipient mentation. Can the infant at the breast, in early stages, be said to have "inner" experiences? In posing such a question, we are asking in terms that themselves distinguish between inner and outer. There are good reasons to assume that this distinction, together with a host of other distinctions (among them, between past and present, here and there, physical and psychical), gradually evolves from a kind of unitary, global experience. This unitary experience perhaps may best be called *being,* if we do not immediately think of it as contrasted with "having been," "becoming," "having," or "doing."

We know states of identification where the boundaries between self and object world, between oneself and another person, are blurred or tend to vanish. In the early stages of human life, it seems, such boundaries are not yet established. We are not born with such discriminations, they develop gradually, becoming more or less firmly fixed in the course of childhood. The older, nondiscriminating forms of experience persist behind the more advanced ones. They may come to the fore under certain exceptional conditions: in psychosis, in situations of deep intimacy between people, in some drug-related and in ecstatic states. The intimacy of the infant-mother unity or bond is the prototype. While the mother functions on several levels of experience, at once or successively, the infant, we assume, in early stages functions more or less exclusively on the identificatory level of experience. Since, objectively, there is no identity of baby and mother—physical enclosure in the mother before birth does not even qualify—one is led to call this identity and identification a mental or imaginative act. It is instinctual in the sense that such mental acts are unmodulated and nondifferentiating.

Given a reasonably attuned mother, both mother and baby share and participate in such experience. It is not just one or the other who experiences in this mode, and we have reason to believe that disturbances in psychic life result if these shared experiences are interfered with. Insofar as there is identity or identification, the objectively other person is not an object for a subject; there is no relationship but sameness. This primordial type of experience is not unique to the mother-infant matrix. It, or its direct derivatives, are encountered in various forms in adult experience. But there they ordinarily are overshadowed by more highly organized forms of experience and are often denied or broken off due to the development of anxiety. Such experiences are often felt as threats to individuality, to the ego's cohesion and stability, but they may also lead to blissful exaltation. They seem to be involved in truly creative work. Similar forms of mentation are known to us from ethnopsychological research and studies in comparative and developmental psychology. They have, among other non-differentiating features, an atemporal, ahistorical character, as though what we call history and historicity, as distinguished from myth, begins or is connected with the differentiated, hierarchical structuring of complex forms of mentation.

In the early stages of psychoanalysis attention was focused on object libido and its vicissitudes; its prototype was seen in the child's love life at the oedipal stage of psychosexual development. Having outlined an early form of love in the mother-infant situation—which may be called a love-matrix—we must state that object libido is a comparatively late form. In contrast to the early, identificatory form of love, object libido refers to acts wherein what is cathected or needed is objectified. Object libido is objectifying libido. In and by this libidinal act, what is desired is structured as another, as an object different from the desire and the desiring agent. In early infancy, it seems, in contrast to this objectification, mouth and breast, the need and the needed, the mother's existence and the infant's, a mother's contentment and an infant's quietude, the mother's and the infant's tension or anxiety, are not differentiated. In adult life emotions and moods still have a tendency to be similarly "contagious."

Here we are in the area of narcissistic libido. Narcissistic libido, in the strict sense of that term, knows no such distinctions. More definitive differentiation between an ego and other "objects" (including the differentiation among different objects), is an advance in mental complexity that leads, as seen from the instinctual-affective side, gradually to the oedipal phase. This is complemented and promoted by a congenial, attuned gradual change of parental attitudes and feelings toward the child.

Freud postulated a primary stage of narcissism where the libido would still be contained, as it were, in the primitive ego. In the course of the development of object relations—a development that takes place in the conjunction of infantile and parental experiential changes and exchanges—this libido is then partially "transferred" to objects. A portion of the original narcissistic libido remains within the ego.

But as the differentiation of ego and objects does not exist in the earliest stages, primary narcissism must be understood without reference to what we call libido attachment or distribution within the ego—as well as without speaking of libido attachments to objects. There is as yet neither ego nor object. We may speak of an undifferentiated force field which later becomes differentiated into ego and objects.[12]

From here we can understand how our love life develops in such a way that one main current desires and longs for other persons as objects of desire, while the other, more ancient current remains "narcissistic" in the sense that it does not recognize boundaries between ego and objects, it creates identity of ego and object. In such identification the subject–object differentiation is suspended or is not activated. It is in this fashion that the ego may enrich itself and "take into itself" aspects or traits of others. In early childhood this process plays a prominent part in ego formation and consolidation; but it continues, in far more complex ways, in later developmental stages as well, especially in superego development.

12. The paradoxical concept of narcissistic object choice (S. Freud, "On Narcissism: An Introduction," *S.E.*, 14:69–102) refers to later stages of an individual's love life where the love object may be chosen on the basis of strong resemblance to oneself (14:88).

Love, then, is a force or power that not only brings people together, one person loving another, but equally brings oneself together into that one individuality which we become through our identifications. Once the differentiation between ego and object is reasonably well established on one level of our mental life, once there is some sort of self-identity as distinguished from the identity of others, we are able to love ourselves as we are able to love another, each different from the other. Thus object-love and self-love (as well as hatred of others and self-hate) develop together.

Self-love, often also called narcissism, must be distinguished from that identificatory love which, as I expressed it, brings one together into one individual self. In self-love, love *of* self, a stage is reached where one becomes an object to oneself, where one can respond to and care for oneself. This involves a split *within* the subject that is analogous to that other split, the ego–object distinction. In the development of object-love the object—needed, longed and cared for—is increasingly appreciated as an ego, a subject in its own right with its own needs and cares, similar to oneself. Equally, in the development of love of self, one's own ego, needful and caring, is more and more appreciated as an object to oneself, needed and to be cared for. Superego development is a related issue.

Love of self may be described as a form of secondary narcissism. It is secondary insofar as it arises only on the basis of that primary, identificatory form of love which leads to the *formation* of an ego. It is secondary also insofar as that duality, that split within the subject, by which love of self comes into being, occurs.

It may be recalled from the first lecture that the development of preconscious or conscient mentation is based on a similar splitting whereby a unitary, unconscious, mental process differentiates so that a mutual responding, an inner *conscire* may result. In psychoanalytic theory, unconscious and preconscious mental processes are distinguished as primary and secondary process. Again, primary and secondary here refer both to a temporal sequence in development, and to the difference between a unitary and a dual mental process. Splitting, duality, and multiplicity make possible a *conscire*, a knowing together.

We can now link the unconscious or id to narcissistic or identificatory libido. This libido is unitary in the same sense in which unconscious mentation is unitary. Equally, we can link consciousness or ego to object libido, that love which objectifies, where loving and that which is loved are distinguished in the act of loving. (I believe that Lacan's idea of the ego as a structure of alienation is related to the splitting in which duality becomes established.)

Narcissistic and object libido, identification and object-cathexis, unconscious and conscious—these pairs now appear to refer to the two currents in the unfolding and organization of man's love life, of his relatedness to the world and himself. What in one perspective we call cognition and ideation, perceiving and knowing, in the present perspective is man's affective instinctual life, his love life. It is our conscient, secondary form of mentation that establishes the distinction between ideation and affectivity. When I speak of mentation *or* experience, as though synonymous, I intend to indicate the fundamental unity of these psychic activities prior to, and as the basis of, secondary distinctions. In action the two sides come together again.

Narcissism—to sum up—in my discussion does not refer primarily to love of self in contrast to love of others, but to that primordial love-mentation which does not structure or divide reality into the poles of inner and outer, subject and object, self and other, any more than the dynamic unconscious does. If left to its own devices, not tempered by secondary process and object-love, it leads to chaos and self-destruction.

Object-love and love of self are forms of love that develop on the basis of narcissism. I went into a discussion of narcissism to show one aspect of the genesis and history of the individual's love life. This could not be done without some discussion of the history of the individual qua individual, because the process of individuation in an important sense *is* the development of his love life from its primitive roots in the infant-mother unity. In reference to this unitary libidinal field, and in view of the interaction processes within it, the term "primordial (or primary) transference" has come into use. One can speak here of transference insofar as libidinal transactions take place in this field. It is a very general use of the term. In the same general sense, but on the level of object libido, we speak of transference in reference to object relations and to the rapport between patient and analyst, insofar as a transactional field is established.

In the narrower, more specific sense of the term, transference refers to the historical dimension of love, to the historical determination and stratification of love relations. When I speak of love relations and of man's love life, it should be understood that I include in the term all its different variations, vicissitudes, and ramifications, including its opposite, hate, and all those forms of intense or passionate feelings and actions that are viewed as negative or destructive. I cannot in this context go into the complex problems of aggression which in Freud's later thought tended to gain a status coequal with libido (rather than as a derivative or form of the latter), considerations which influenced to a considerable extent his late instinct theory. The problem of so-called negative transference is a related issue.

Transference first came into view in the psychoanalytic treatment situation. It was found that the transference—in the general sense—that the patient developed toward the analyst consisted of, or was greatly determined by, earlier love–hate relationships, ultimately those that arose in the first flowering of object relations in the oedipal period. Many of the neurotic problems of patients could be traced back to emotional conflicts, and defenses against them, that first arose in the intimate object relations of the oedipal period. If these early object relations, for a variety of reasons, have not undergone further development in the postoedipal period and adolescence, then later love relations remain determined by the unmodified power of those prototypes. This can be clearly observed under the special conditions of the psychoanalytic situation, in the transference to the analyst, who becomes for the patient a representative of the parental objects of the oedipal past.

I have spoken of that more ancient current of love, narcissistic love, where boundaries between ego or self and object are not recognized or become blurred; this current harks back to the stage of primary narcissism. Increased understanding of narcissism has led to a widening of our horizon in regard to the depth of the historical determination and stratification of man's love life. Compared to that early, narcissistic form of love, the prototype of which is the mother-infant unit, oedipal love, object-love, is a late stage, which in normal psychosexual development increasingly overshadows and dominates the psychic scene. Nevertheless, that original current does not disappear. In fact it exerts an essential influence on further, postoedipal development of psychic life and object relations. Freud has referred to this development as the dissolution of the Oedipus complex, leading to the formation of the superego. It is the enriched complexity of psychic life, brought about by the internalization of elements of oedipal relations, that makes possible the more mature love relations of adult life. Internalization involved in super-ego development can be described as a narcissistic transformation of object relations. Interactions between child and parents during the oedipal period are trans-formed into internal, intrapsychic interactions and relations. This does not mean, of course, that relations with the parents and other objects cease, but that object world and object relations gain further depth and new dimensions by virtue of a reorganization of the inner life.

The organization of the inner life, of the internal world, and its further reorganizations in the course of development, are topics I cannot discuss to any extent in this context. Let me say only this: the narcissistic retransformations of object relations, involved in internalization on the level of superego development, are, at least in part, induced and promoted by the increasing separateness of child and parents. Processes of separation and emancipation from each other occur in both, child and parents, in mutually determined phases. Mourning is a psychic activity that comprises the relinquishment of intimate object relations and the reestablishment, in the internal arena, of elements of these object relations by identificatory processes. In mourning, an object relationship is gradually given up, involving pain and suffering, and is substituted by a restructuring of the internal world which is in consonance with the relinquished relationship. In this way pain and suffering can eventually cease, even while the memories of the lost person do remain. Increased separateness and distance between child and parents are part of normal development and always involve experiences of loss, although not only of loss. But the sense of increased inner freedom that goes with emancipation from parents and parental figures is connected with this narcissistic, internal reconstitution. Such losses are only healed by further individuation. In this sense one can say that individuation of the individual comes about by the losses of separation. Superego development through what Freud has called the destruction of the Oedipus complex is the paradigm.

Transference in the psychoanalytic situation shows special characteristics, partly due to the unique features and purposes of the analytic process, and partly because of each patient's pathology. But the historical determination and stratification of the individual's love life is universal. What varies greatly is the degree to which our early love life, in its narcissistic and object-libidinal dimensions, manages to develop into more mature forms and expressions, and to what degree our love life remains fixated at, or is easily thrown back to, early levels.

I hope to have made it clear that in psychic development early levels do not disappear, and that later stages are not to be misconstrued as simply early stages in disguise—as though they were camouflaged in order to go unnoticed or to be acceptable to our defensive requirements.

It is true, however, that our repressive-defensive tendencies or needs, which interfere with genuine psychic development, frequently operate in that way; what passes for maturity then is closer to repressed infantilism. Such disguises, often not discrete neurotic symptoms but characterological traits, operate in everybody.

You notice that I said, *operate in everybody*. This implies that it is not we who defend, but something, some so-called defense *mechanism*, impersonal forces. With the following considerations I return to an earlier theme. It is precisely the recognition, the acknowledgment that such "mechanisms," such forces, are, or will become, our own, and may be appropriated—it is this potentiality for appropriation which constitutes the individual's moral propensity and which psychoanalytic interpretations use. Psychoanalysis acknowledges the impersonal or nonpersonal beginnings and levels of psychic life; to own up to this, to make them one's own, is man's evolutionary task—to create oneself as a person by taking these beginnings over and into an individual life-continuum. Nonpersonal psychic forces, seen from an ego perspective or from the vantage point of personal life, are potentially ours. In regard to defenses, the question is whether we are to be ruled by them or whether we can flexibly use them, in the haste and urgency of everyday life. Unconscious defenses, as unconscious, are direct counterparts to unconscious instinctual forces; they grow in the same soil. In the moral movement of which I spoke, both become personalized, are re-created as personal; in our responsiveness they become our responsibility. In this deep sense it is not our responsibility to render our so-called immoral or amoral impulses or libidinal needs inoffensive to the world's and our own official morality and to repress them, but to raise them to the level of our current life context, to integrate them into adult ego-organization. Responsible action and responsible thought would have some such meaning. In this sense we are called upon to make our own history.

Our early love life is repeated during our life—whether or not we recognize it, in its more or less infantile guises and disguises, or in more mature forms—often in both at the same time or alternately. Repetition may be a reiteration of the same, an automatic, driven reenactment of early relationships. This is neurotic or pathological transference. But repetition also may be a re-creation, an imaginative reorganization and elaboration of the early, life-giving love experiences—troublesome, frustrating, and full of conflict as most of them have been. Kierkegaard has spoken of "the dialectic of repetition": "what is repeated has been, otherwise it could not be repeated, but precisely the fact that it has been gives to *repetition* the character of novelty."[13]

13. S. Kierkegaard, *Repetition: An Essay in Experimental Psychology* (1843). Princeton, N.J.: Princeton University Press, 1946, p. 34. The sentence following the above quotation is

This understanding of repetition, emphasizing the aspect of novelty and active re-creation of the past in the present, is implicit in the formula that id shall become ego. It reveals transference in its nonpathological meaning, as the dynamic of psychological growth and development. The concept of transference, in this sense, underlines our historical continuity in development and change. This is far from reductionism.

But to the extent to which the repetitions of transference remain or revert to unconsciously driven reiteration of the past, to that extent the individual *is* reduced in his love-life and in the other dimensions of mental life, regardless of intelligence. Transference does not mean that we are condemned to mindless re-enactment of early love relations. Nor does conscious understanding of automatic repetitions, of unconscious transference manifestations, lead to the elimination of transference. Consciousness of transference means that the living interpenetration of inner past and present can be resumed. In *The Interpretation of Dreams* Freud spoke of transference in terms of a need for attachment between unconscious and preconscious, of a "play" between them.[14] It is this interplay between unconscious and consciousness, between past and

_____

significant: "When the Greeks said that all knowledge is recollection they affirmed that all that is has been; when one says that life is a repetition one affirms that existence which has been now becomes."

14. *The Interpretation of Dreams. S.E.,* 5:564. See also *ibid.,* 562–63.

present, between the intense density of undifferentiated, inarticulate experience and the lucidity of
conscious articulate experience, that gives meaning to
our life. Without such meaning-giving play we have no
future of our own. Perhaps what we call man's sym-
bolizing activity is that play.

Psychoanalytic interpretations, in the most precise
sense of that term, have no other aim than to activate
or rekindle this symbol-forming libidinal spark in the
patient. In interactions with the loved and hated analyst,
a blend of narcissistic and object libido, under propitious
circumstances the patient is enabled to transmute
received interpretations into internally active insight.
Through the communications between patient and
analyst, each being moved by the other, that internal
movement and communication may be reactivated
which Freud has described as transference between
unconscious and preconscious.

Psychoanalysis, in its doctrine of transference, tells us
that adult love relations contain at their genetic core the
early bonds (and the inherent frustrations and disrup-
tions) by which human mental life comes into being
and first develops. An articulate understanding of these
connections and stratifications can help us to construct
our inner history, and become active agents in its
future course. Inner history does not mean merely
reconstruction of past objective events or subjective
experiences, but aware appropriation of the interplay

and communication between unconscious and conscious modes of mentation and desire. In creating higher awareness of the psychic fabric of our individuality, psychoanalysis is adding a new dimension and a new tension and purposefulness to our historicity.

III

Comments on
Religious Experience

In the two previous lectures I have tried to give some account of the historicity of the individual. I have taken the view that individuation proceeds by increasing differentiation and emancipation from a primary matrix, typified in human life by the original infant-mother psychic unit. We come to live in objectified reality by virtue, basically, of the development of secondary process mentation which is tied to processes and events of differentiation and separation. The psychic reality of the infant in early stages lacks the various distinctions and discriminations by which we come to organize our world and orient ourselves in it. Indeed, it makes sense to say that the world, including ourselves, becomes a world of ours by the stepwise separations and differentiations from an unstructured uniformity which, to the extent of our knowledge, is first interfered with by the event of birth. As our psychic life develops, we appropriate, own up to this event and its far-reaching consequences. Sexual differentiation, the fact that one is born male or female, and that one is conceived by sexual intercourse between male and female and grows

up in a world of males and females and a sexually
differentiated family, is another of those givens that it
becomes our evolutionary task to take over as ours, to
be responsive to.

The distinction between primary and secondary
process in psychic life is fundamental. This distinction
comes from the growing awareness and articulation in
modern consciousness of the fact that the conscient
forms of mentation with which we are so familiar and
at home especially in our scientific age are founded on,
and are a further differentiation of, mental processes of
a more ancient cast. The latter are closer to the origins
of mental life in the instinctual, single-minded life of
the race and the emerging individual. They are, or
represent, our past as mentating beings. But they are not
only "past history," something we have overcome or are
bound to put behind us. These unconscious forms of
mentation or experience are with us now. We would
lose ourselves in a chaos—different from the formless-
ness of the unconscious or id, a chaos of fragmentation
instead—if we were to lose our moorings in the unconscious and its forms of experiencing which bespeak
unity and identity rather than multiplicity and difference. We know madness that is the madness of un-
bridled rationality. Secondary process mentation is an
achievement of the highest order, but it must be seen as
a continuous activity of the mind, not as a static state
reached once and for all. If we do not evolve it again
and again from the primary form of mentation and
return to and evolve from the latter again, rational

thought becomes sterile and destructive of life, as it denies or ignores its own living source.

I believe that some aspects of religious experience are related to unconscious mental processes. Other aspects of religious life and thought can be approached by interpreting them in terms of the emergent dialectic between unconscious and conscient mentation, roughly speaking, between the irrational and the rational. What I have to say about these matters is tentative and fragmentary and will not lead very far. But I hope it may lead a step beyond what psychoanalysis has contributed so far to the understanding—and misunderstanding—of religion. Here, as elsewhere in psychoanalysis, Freud has laid some groundwork. But he deliberately did not pursue his basic hunches, and under the weight of his authority religion in psychoanalysis has been largely considered as a sign of man's mental immaturity, of his need for finding rather transparent substitutes for his infantile dependency on parental protection against the threats and frustrations of life. The need for protection by an all-powerful father remained for Freud the basic fact that led to the creation of religion. He professed to be at a loss even to explain the existence of mother goddesses that presumably preceded the existence of father gods in archaic religions.

Freud's well-known view on religion is that it is an illusion, comforting to the child in us, to the "common man," an illusion to be given up as we are able to overcome our childish needs for all-powerful parents. In essence, the ideas of "God" and of an eternal life are

consolations or defenses—to help man cope with the
exigencies, frustrations, and transitoriness of human
life. What "the common man understands by his religion," Freud, in *Civilization and Its Discontents* (1930),
describes as follows:

> the system of doctrines and promises which on the
> one hand explains to him the riddles of this world
> with enviable completeness, and, on the other, assures
> him that a careful Providence will watch over his life
> and will compensate him in a future existence for any
> frustrations he suffers here. The common man cannot
> imagine this Providence otherwise than in the figure
> of an enormously exalted father. Only such a being
> can understand the needs of the children of men and
> be softened by their prayers and placated by the signs
> of their remorse. The whole thing is so patently in-
> fantile, so foreign to reality, that to anyone with a
> friendly attitude to humanity it is painful to think
> that the great majority of mortals will never be able
> to rise above this view of life.[15]

But prodded by his friend Romain Rolland, the
French writer whom he greatly admired, Freud admitted in the same book that he had perhaps not concerned himself with "the deepest sources of the religious
feeling." Rolland, in response to Freud's *The Future of
an Illusion* (1927), had objected to Freud's one-sided
understanding of religion as an illusion or form of
childhood neurosis. According to Freud's account in

15. *S.E.*, 21:74.

the first chapter of *Civilization and Its Discontents,*
Rolland maintained that

> The true source of religious sentiments . . . consists
> in a peculiar feeling, which he [Rolland] himself is
> never without, which he finds confirmed by many
> others, and which he may suppose is present in mil-
> lions of people. It is a feeling which he would like to
> call a sensation of "eternity," a feeling as of some-
> thing limitless, unbounded—as it were, "oceanic."
> This feeling, he adds, is a purely subjective fact, not
> an article of faith; it brings with it no assurance of
> personal immortality, but it is the source of the
> religious energy which is seized upon by various
> Churches and religious systems, directed by them into
> particular channels, and doubtless also exhausted by
> them. One may, he thinks, rightly call oneself religious
> on the ground of this oceanic feeling alone, even if
> one rejects every belief and every illusion.[16]

Freud continues that he cannot discover this oceanic
feeling in himself and that for this and other reasons he
can approach this subject only with misgivings and
hesitations. In his own description, such a sentiment
would be

> a feeling of an indissoluble bond, of being one with
> the external world as a whole. . . . The idea of men's
> receiving an intimation of their connection with the
> world around them through an immediate feeling,
> oriented from the outset toward that *Umwelt,* sounds
> so strange and fits in so badly with the fabric of our

16. *Ibid.,* p. 64.

psychology that one is justified in attempting to discover a psychoanalytic—that is, a genetic—derivation of such a feeling.[17]

He then proceeds, in effect, to derive that feeling from the primary narcissistic unity of the infant-mother psychic matrix and sketches the early development of the adult's ego feeling from its primitive beginnings in such a matrix, focusing on the growing differentiation between an ego, an inside, and an outside world. He also mentions that "At the height of being in love the boundary between ego and object threatens to melt away," and that there are pathological states in which the boundaries between ego and external world tend to vanish or to be incorrectly drawn.[18] Freud concludes:

Our present ego-feeling is, therefore, only a shrunken residue of a much more inclusive—indeed, an all-embracing—feeling which corresponded to a more intimate bond between the ego and the world about it [Umwelt]. If we may assume that there are many people in whose mental life this primary ego-feeling has persisted to a greater or less degree, it would exist in them side by side with the narrower and more sharply demarcated ego-feeling of maturity, like a kind of counterpart to it. In that case, the ideational contents appropriate to it would be precisely those of limitlessness and of a bond with the universe—the same ideas with which my friend [Rolland] elucidated the "oceanic" feeling.[19]

17. *Ibid.*, p. 65 (translation slightly modified).
18. *Ibid.*, p. 66.
19. *Ibid.*, p. 68.

Freud here speaks of the coexistence of primitive and later developmental stages of mentation, a subject we have previously discussed as appropriation and transference. And I have suggested that the range and richness of human life is directly proportional to the mutual responsiveness between these various mental phases and levels. It should be added that what seems primitive or archaic about such early phases loses that character if not seen in isolation or merely from the standpoint of conscient mentation and rational thought. While the latter is a later development, it limits and impoverishes—Freud speaks of a shrunken vestige—the perspective, understanding, and range of human action, feeling, and thought, unless it is brought back into coordination and communication with those modes of experience that remain their living source, and perhaps their ultimate destination. It is not a foregone conclusion that man's objectifying mentation is, or should be, an ultimate end rather than a component and intermediate phase of vital significance to us.

In his account of the development of "ego-feeling" from its origins in primary narcissism, Freud focused on the growing distinction between the ego and the outer world, between internal and external. But there arises an equal if not more basic differentiation in the unfolding of mental life—that of temporal modes. The concept of eternity, mentioned by Rolland and Freud in connection with the "oceanic" feeling, has reference to time.

Eternity[20] is generally considered a religious concept. It is conceived as the counterpart to history and time, as encompassing, transcending, or annihilating time. It seems that eternity and time are correlative concepts and that ultimately one cannot be thought of without reference to the other. I am not concerned here with the philosophy of time or eternity. Both concepts have arisen in the human mind. Although we do not understand time, we can relate the concept to a great variety of our experiences and can assume that secondary process mentation itself would be unthinkable without temporal categories of some kind. Kant, in investigating the organization of conscious mentation, held the view that time, by way of schemata that underlie our sensible concepts, conveys the most fundamental outlines of organization to the material of experience. Time, although somehow incomprehensible since it seems to be at the root of what we call comprehensibility and understanding, is familiar to us in many different contexts, and we can easily think in terms of experiencing time. But what about eternity? Is there anything like an experience of eternity in human life?

Eternity has to be distinguished from sempiternity or everlastingness. Everlastingness, unending duration, conveys of course the idea of time unlimited, unending time, perhaps time that has no beginning and no end.

20. For the following discussion of eternity, cf. my paper, "The Experience of Time," in R. S. Eissler et al, eds., *The Psychoanalytic Study of the Child*. New York: Quadrangle Books, 1972, 27:401–410.

We have experiences of time being interminable, as when we are bored. Compared with the short lifespan of the individual, with its sharply delimited beginning and end, the course of history or the life of the race seems unending and without a clear beginning. The idea of sempiternity, of everlasting duration, was for a long time best exemplified by the revolutions of the stars and astronomical motion. Whatever seemed incommensurate with human time dimensions and measurements, even in the aggregate of human experience, was and still is experienced as everlasting, although we may now know otherwise.

Eternity, on the other hand, is not time that has no limit. The category of time does not apply, except in contrast. In the experience of eternity, time is abolished. The articulation of experience in terms of temporal modes—past, present, and future—and in terms of duration, change, succession, and simultaneity, is not universal in human experience. Empathic observation of young infants suggests that they do not experience "in time," that they do not experience time, although their experiences, movements, and actions, do objectively occur in time. In early stages of development, there does not seem to be anything like a past, present, or future. Experience appears to be, in the words of William James, a buzzing, blooming confusion. It seems likely that the articulation of experience in terms of these temporal modes ushers in the beginning of higher, secondary forms of mentation. What we call advanced mentation appears to imply such differentiations, which may come earlier and be more crucial than spatial distinctions.

We know of exceptional and pathological states where the sense of time is "suspended." States of this kind have been described by mystics. Similar conditions have been described by perceptive self-observers to obtain in ecstatic states under the influence of certain drugs. In emotional states of exceptional intensity, in orgastic experiences, in the height of bliss or the depth of despair, the temporal attributes of experience fall away; only a "now," outside time, remains.

In retrospect, these moments or periods, having occurred in a time that can be measured, tend to be described as timeless, as though time stood still. If we speak of this as an illusion, we are speaking from the perspective of developed temporality, in terms of secondary process mentation. This form of mentation dominates our waking-life awareness, and it determines our reporting of dreams, although in dreams we may discern elements of timelessness. From the standpoint of that timelessness, that is, from the dream perspective itself, what we call, by means of conscious mentation, the actual sequence of dream events, one after the other, may feel to us as a falsification. Our discursive language is hardly adequate to render the condensation that may take place in a dream where time collapses. Neither the felt version nor the verbalized version, it seems to me, should be called an illusion. If we acknowledge the undifferentiating unconscious as a genuine mode of mentation which underlies and unfolds into secondary process mentation (and remains extant together with it, although concealed by it), then we regain a more comprehensive perspective—no doubt with its own limitations yet unknown. Such a perspective betokens a new level of consciousness, of conscire, on which primary and secondary modes of mentation may be known together.

Philosophers and theologians have spoken of the *nunc stans,* the abiding now, the instant that knows no temporal articulation, where distinctions between now, earlier, and later have fallen away or have not arisen. All of us know, I believe, poignant moments that have this timeless quality: unique and matchless, complete in themselves and somehow containing all there is in experience. As experience augments and grows in an individual's life course, these instants, *in* time but not *of* time, contain more and more meaning which is poured into the *nunc stans* in such a way that temporal and other articulating differentiations are dissolved or become condensed into oneness. What was lived through earlier and later, and the mental categories of secondary process mentation—all fall away, collapsing into an instant, into that one experience which then stands for all experience, although only "for one instant."

It is no accident that the idea of condensation comes up here. In psychoanalytic theory, condensation is the main characteristic of the primary process. The primary process in pure form is, I believe, extant in the experience of eternity.

I have mentioned in my discussion of transference

those instances when, in the intense focus of the psychoanalytic process, something is re-experienced, in relation
to the analyst, that occurred in childhood in relation to
a parent. We say that the memory is so vivid that past
and present are no longer distinguished. Similar things
may occur, of course, outside the analytic situation. A
person gets lost, as we say, in memories of his or her
past life with someone beloved who died, a parent,
friend, husband, wife, a child. Often such memories
are triggered by a current experience. The more we let
ourselves be affected by them, the less we simply recall
them in actuarial fashion as events that took place at
one time—and the more we relive them in a *now* that is
not distinguished as present from past.

I have mentioned the distinction between remembering and repeating, when speaking of unconscious memory. In poignant remembering, in a remembering that
moves us, the difference between recollecting and
repeating diminishes. As we become absorbed in such
memories not only do we lose, as we say, the sense of
time and space, but we tend to repeat, relive, internally
and in our imagination, what we perhaps wanted only
to recall as past events. And while we may repeat in
temporal sequence, while we may go through these
experiences again step by step, the index of pastness
recedes or vanishes. At times, in such remembering,
these experiences take on a prototypical significance, as
though they easily might stand for all experience, as
though in them could be represented or fulfilled the
essence, the sum total of our life, in archetypal form.

We get lost in the contemplation of a beautiful scene, or face, or painting, in listening to music, or poetry, or the music of a human voice. We are carried away in the vortex of sexual passion. We become absorbed in the proportions of a building, the plastic force or harmony of a sculpture, in a deeply stirring play or film, in the beauty of a scientific theory or experiment, or of an animal, in the intimate closeness of a personal encounter. In all such experiences, while our rational processes may continue to operate and to articulate the material of experience, at the same time another level of our mind has been touched and activated, and the secondary, rational form of mentation loses its weight. It is overshadowed or pervaded by the timelessness of the unconscious or primary process. Once the experience is over, we can of course try to grasp and keep hold of it in terms of secondary process mentation.

The *nunc stans,* approximated in experiences of this kind, the staying-power of such experiences, tends to be expressed in analogical. terms by comparing it with nonending time, everlastingness. The idea of eternity has often been made concrete in religious terms as everlasting life after death. That eternity is represented in this fashion is, I believe, due to the influence of secondary process mentation. Using such mentation, as we ordinarily do, the expression "everlasting life after death" is the closest we can come to the representation of eternity. Individual life has a beginning and an end, it takes place in time; it is likely that our idea of time and the temporal articulation of our experience is in some way intimately connected with our knowledge of death. On the other hand, Freud thought that the unconscious has no conception of death, and that the id is "timeless."

The fact that such experiences are timeless implies that they are structured or centered differently, that beginning and ending, temporal succession and simultaneity, are not part of them. They are transtemporal in their inner fabric. The idea of duration, everlasting or not, plays no part in them.

The concept of eternity—as a counterpart to time, and not as a limitless extension of time—has arisen, I believe, from such and related experiences. Freud, in the text I quoted earlier, pointed to the genetic derivation of this conception, and he did not deny Rolland's claim, which to me is valid, that such an ego feeling, as Freud called it, may be at the root of religious experience.

States or experiences of this kind manifest forms of mentation that seem to be blends of primary and secondary process. They only rarely occur in adult life in a more purely primary form, or awareness of such pure forms is rare. In childhood they seem to be more prominent and frequent. They are best described or represented in poetic forms in which our language, so dominated in ordinary life and even more in scientific discourse by secondary process mentation, is drawn into the force field of the primary process. Considering this, Freud's notion that "word presentations," by becoming connected with "unconscious thing presentations," transform primary into secondary process, does not appear to do full justice to the potentialities and to the origins of language.

Psychoanalysts tend to consider the idea of eternity, religious experiences connected with it, as well as the "timeless" experiences I described, in pragmatic fashion as useful and often necessary defenses, or as mental sanctuaries people must have to cope with the fear of death, castration, and with the trials, tribulations, and the transitoriness of human life. I do not doubt the truth of this view. But it is not the whole truth. I believe that "intimations of eternity" bring us in touch with levels of our being, forms of experiencing and of reality that themselves may be deeply disturbing, anxiety provoking to the common-sense rationality of everyday life. They go against our penchant for objectifying and distancing our experience and our world in order to make and keep it manageable and tolerable. As we grow up the more we become involved in the business of living, and conducting a responsible and rational life, the more we find safety in the sense of order and personal power that the active conduct and direction of a reasonably successful life can give. Conscious forms of mentation are primarily—at least so it appears—responsible for our success and achievement, our domination of the forces of nature, our control over others and over ourselves. Seen from this angle, our unconscious forms of mentation are, in a non-metaphysical sense, unworldly. They evince another mode of reality. I am not speaking of a realm of Being beyond or above this universe, of a spiritual world located elsewhere, but of a different form of reality as organizing experience. This form is more-or-less ignored in modern Western thought, insofar as we are dominated by a narrow scientism.

At this point I would like to quote a passage from a talk given in London in the early nineteen-fifties by the physicist J. Robert Oppenheimer, entitled "Uncommon Sense":

> Transience is the backdrop for the play of human progress, for the improvement of man, the growth of his knowledge, the increase of his power, his corruption and his partial redemption. Our civilizations perish; the carved stone, the written word, the heroic act fade into a memory of memory and in the end are gone. The day will come when our race is gone; this house, this earth in which we live will one day be unfit for human habitation, as the sun ages and alters.
>
> Yet no man, be he agnostic or Buddhist or Christian, thinks wholly in these terms. His acts, his thoughts, what he sees of the world around him—the falling of a leaf or a child's joke or the rise of the moon—are part of history; but they are not only part of history; they are part of becoming and of process but not only that; they also partake of the world outside of time; they partake of the light of eternity.[21]

Some of you may think that it is a sign of my age to concern myself with such matters as religion and eter-

21. J. R. Oppenheimer, *Science and the Common Understanding*. New York: Simon & Schuster, 1954, pp. 68-82.

nity. Let me say a few words about that. There is no doubt that a good many people, including myself, tend to become more involved in such questions as they advance in age. Age in general influences the areas and the range of one's interests, observations, and thought. At any given age during the course of one's life, one is likely to be more open to certain areas of experience and knowledge than to others, more involved in some and less involved in others. Areas of experience previously ignored or given little weight may move into the center, while others may recede. But as far as I can see no rules can be established. A great many young people, perhaps more than people in middle age, are concerned with some of the problems I raised. Many of the ideas I am discussing tonight have been on my mind for years. Age may have given me greater freedom to voice them in public. But whatever the variations of individual interest according to age, they do not say anything about the general validity or importance in human life of the different spheres and forms of experience.

It is my belief that the distinction between conscious —more precisely between preconscious or conscient— and unconscious mentation, rightly understood, places psychoanalytic psychology in the position of shedding new light on important aspects of religious experience. Under the dominating influence of Freud's views on religion, psychoanalysis has shied away from this task. Freud did not recognize (or refused to recognize) that religious life, as anything else in human life, is capable of evolving more mature forms of functioning and expression, no less than human love, for example. Understanding such maturity involves understanding in depth the interplay of conscious and unconscious knowledge. Freud—as my earlier quotation from *Civilization and Its Discontents* shows—tangled somewhat with the problem and abandoned it quickly. The dominant currents of psychoanalysis never developed the line of thought whereby religious experience, primary narcissism, and the unconscious were tied together. Jung, as far as I can make out, tended to get lost in what Freud once, in a letter to him, called "your religious-libidinal cloud." Freud, by avoiding a further understanding of religion, remained in this respect on the safe ground of the rational ego, although he did so much to clarify its irrational sources and aspects.

It may be that Freud was greatly conflicted about these matters. In Jung's view there was a deeply religious strain in Freud's conception of the unconscious, a strain Freud could not admit—perhaps we may say he was compelled to repress it—in part because of his aversion and distrust of systematized or institutional religion. Jung thought that Freud's psychosexuality, the *fons et origo* of the unconscious, had the significance of a *deus absconditus,* a God below instead of a God above.[22] We are led to think here of the motto to *The*

22. C. G. Jung, *Memories, Dreams, Reflections.* New York: Pantheon Books, 1961, p. 151.

Interpretation of Dreams: "If I cannot bend the powers above, I shall move those of the netherworld."

If we are willing to admit that instinctual life and religious life both betoken forms of experience that underlie and go beyond conscious and personalized forms of mentation—beyond those forms of mental life, of ordering our world, on which we stake so much —then we may be at a point where psychoanalysis can begin to contribute in its own way to the understanding of religious experience, instead of ignoring or rejecting its genuine validity or treating it as a mark of human immaturity.

Psychoanalysis is depth psychology. Freud, despite his increasing emphasis on and preference for the rational ego, never repudiated that title for his psychology. As depth psychology, it has a twofold task: to make use of our conscious, differentiating, and objectifying mentation to understand more about that other, unconscious form of mentation from which our more complex mental processes derive (and which remains a living and vital resource and component of our mental life); and, in a countermovement, psychoanalysis aims to reconstruct, on the basis of its grasp of unconscious processes, the intricacies and vicissitudes of the organization of conscious life, that is, the ways in which unconscious libidinal forces, motivations, and aims engender or culminate in ego organization, making possible the conduct of responsible individual life. This is also a highly abstract formulation of what is intended in a clinical psychoanalysis.

Certain forms of religious experience to which I have alluded are aspects of unconscious mentation, aspects that in much of modern civilization are more deeply repressed than "sexuality" is today. In good part thanks to psychoanalysis, sexuality is no longer defended against as it was during the Victorian age. The dimension of human life that we call religious, on the other hand, today is largely unconscious, in the general, nonspecific sense of its remaining under the surface of our scientifically informed mentality. But I believe there are signs of change here too, because of the deep common sources of sexual and religious life.

It is a well-known phenomenon that mystical writers and poets of differing religions have expressed or described their ecstatic experiences in language that is very close to, if not identical with, the language used to describe passionate sexual or intimate erotic experiences and fantasies. The common analytic understanding of this phenomenon is that unacceptable or repressed sexual wishes and fantasies push to the surface and are allowed open expression because the ego has put them on an elevated religious level or placed them in a context that is acceptable to the person's defensive requirements. Perhaps this might be illuminated, in caricature, by a famous scene in one of Charlie Chaplin's movies where he stands on the street in front of an art gallery and intently gazes at the statue of a nude, with all the postures and gestures of an art expert. As long as everybody assumes that he is interested in art and not in voyeuristic sexual pleasure, he can look at the nude without inhibition. Of course, in Chaplin's case, the punishment for this forbidden pleasure follows immediately: as he gracefully steps back to get a more comprehensive view, to obtain an even higher aesthetic appreciation of the work of art, he falls into a coal chute that has opened up in the pavement behind him. I am resisting the temptation to pursue the further possible analytic interpretations of this scene.

There can be no question that some analogous interpretation of religious erotic poetry, in terms of sublimation as a defense, has its validity. The movie scene intends to reveal the hypocrisy that is often only thinly concealed in what passes for sublimation. Sublimation is one of the most obscure and vague concepts in psychoanalysis. It is often held to be a successful defense against unacceptable impulses, a type of defense that finds, for instance in the form of art or religious or scientific activity, cultural sanction and thereby acquires a new worth that separates it from its "lowly" origins. This view of sublimation always smacks of reductionism. It also implies that there is some element of sham or pretension in our greatly valued higher activities, and it would be futile to deny that there is an element of truth in such a debunking view of the marvelous virtues of human endeavors and achievements.

I cannot further discuss sublimation here; it would lead us too far afield, as much as the concept needs clarification and is full of ambiguities and pitfalls that have to do with the corruptibility of human beings which Oppenheimer alluded to. A proper discussion of sublimation would have to involve the complexities of the psychoanalytic concept of defense. I believe there is a thin but perceptible line between sublimation as defense and sublimation—if one chooses to use that term—as a genuine appropriation, to use my term for the responsive interplay between id and ego. The same instinctual, vital forces are employed, I believe, in religious erotic poetry as in sexuality. This goes also for aesthetic pleasure and all forms of creativity, most obvious in many forms of artistic creativity. Sexuality, if not defensively or artificially insulated and drained of the fullness of our mental life—a process that in our culture tends to be initiated in childhood—then can be seen as informing those higher mental activities. There is a continuing, mutual interplay between the instinctual and emotional-ideational sides of life. As the latter differentiates from the former, in given instances such as in religious erotic poetry, the two levels of experience symbolize each other, give increased meaning to one another.

I have discussed aspects of the inner history and historicity of the individual and have, in this last lecture, attempted to juxtapose this historicity with an ahistorical, a timeless dimension of human life. The realm of religious life and thought of course is not limited to mystical and other timeless experiences; the dialectic of history or temporality, and eternity, is itself a central problem in all developed religions and in theology. In this perspective, what I discussed as morality, in terms of owning up, of responsiveness and responsibility, of mutual appropriation of unconscious and conscient modes of experience, can be seen as a religious concern. And the dialectic of id and ego/superego can be understood as paralleling the philosophical-theological or religious dialectic of eternity and temporality.

These lectures perhaps have turned out to be, in the end—far more than they should have been—tentative philosophical reflections on psychoanalysis. Some of the things I have discussed I have wanted to say for a long time. I am most grateful for the opportunity this series has provided, and for your interest.